Before the Buddha Came

Walter A. Fairservis, Jr.

This is an account of life as it was when the great civilizations of the Far East were being born. It describes how people lived in the ancient days of China, Korea, Japan, and Central Asia.

The heart of the Far East is China, which was the first land there to develop civilization. Scientists are only beginning to outline how it began through the evidence given by archaeology and ancient texts. These sources tell the history, legends, traditions, writing, and speech of the remote past.

Like the Chinese, Japanese civilization is rooted in a prehistoric past —a past archaeologists are uncovering in their researches. Long closed to the West, Korea has sometimes been called the "Hermit" kingdom because of its isolation, but it has played a vital role in the Far East as the bridge between China and Japan.

The constant movement of Central Asians over the grasslands and deserts has often changed the course of history and profoundly affected the destinies of Far Eastern nations. The author tells vividly how much all these people contributed to the development of man's civilization.

Walter A. Fairservis, Jr., is professor
and chairman of the Department of
Anthropology and Sociology at Vassar College, Poughkeepsie, New York,
and acting curator of the Eurasian Anthropology Collections at the American Museum of Natural History, New
York. He is the author of *Egypt, Gift of
the Nile* and *Mesopotamia, the Civilization That Rose out of Clay,* among
other books.

BEFORE
THE
BUDDHA
CAME

BEFORE
THE
BUDDHA
CAME

WALTER A. FAIRSERVIS, JR.

Illustrated with photographs and with drawings and maps by
JAN FAIRSERVIS

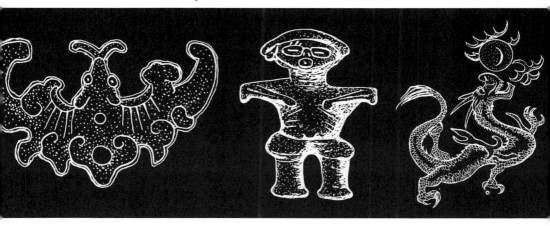

Charles Scribner's Sons
New York

CONTENTS

ILLUSTRATIONS

BEFORE
THE
BUDDHA
CAME

INTRODUCTION
BEYOND SUEZ

Only a hundred years ago when the world was a calmer place the words "east of Suez" used to mean magic, a magic that conjured up dreams of far places where golden cities gleamed and exotic sights pleasured the eye. Young men caught by these visions, desirous of finding wealth or adventure, ventured eastward by land and sea to India and beyond. This "beyond" meant the Far East—the lands of China, Korea, and Japan. The term "Far East" was coined by Englishmen since the western and eastern hemispheres began at Greenwich, England.

In the thirteenth century A.D. the Polo brothers, merchants of Venice, made two trips to Cathay (China); on the second trip they took along Marco, the son of one of them, and it was Marco's account of Cathay that fanned the imaginations of Europeans for centuries. But it was not until the 1600s that Europeans were able to make the long voyage to that land and to Japan with any regularity. Japan then decided to exclude all Europeans, and it was not until the

1

middle of the nineteenth century that foreign visitors to that country were welcome.

Foreigners marveled at the splendors of art; the great statues of wood, stone, and bronze; the exquisite jade and amber carvings; the marvelous lacquer boxes; the mystical paintings and prints; the intricate workmanship in pottery and basketry. In architecture there were palaces and temples as mighty in conception and execution, as rich in ornament, as any in Europe, and yet there were quiet, dignified buildings set in forests or by streams, which blended with their backgrounds as if they were part of the natural world. Such structures had been made without the nails and metal braces that Europeans used as means of fastening plank to beam. All was pegged, grooved, and glued!

In religion and philosophy there were men as wise as those of Europe, and conceptions of god and man which even in our scientific age are studied by sage men. In literature there were novels and poems, epics and legends—a wealth of words expressing the thoughts, beliefs, and experiences of heroes, saints, and ordinary people.

Everywhere the European went he found strange and sometimes terrible things, such as cruel punishment and fatalistic ways of viewing life. But there was one impression that colored his views of the Far East probably more than any other—the feeling of how ancient were the cultures of the Far East. Indeed, he found men who talked of people dead over a thousand years as if they were yet living; he saw people carving ivory, planting rice, and weaving clothes almost exactly as they were depicted on the carved stone walls of ancient temples. Constantly people spoke of the remote past when asked why they did things in certain ways. When they referred to that past they usually meant the times before the coming of Buddhism.

Buddhism, one of the great faiths of the Far East, arose in India and arrived in the Far East when the Roman Empire existed in Europe. The Roman Empire was the last empire of the ancient world. The great empires of Egypt, Mesopotamia, and Persia had collapsed and vanished long before Rome. When Rome flourished the Greeks had had their day and had finally fallen. Christianity was on its way to becoming the principal faith of Rome when Buddhism came to China. It was only about two hundred years before Charlemagne was crowned (A.D. 800) that Buddhism reached Japan.

It is the ancient world of the Far East before Buddhism that concerns us. It was the time when out of the simple life of prehistoric man emerged the splendid Eastern civilizations about which men still think and wonder.

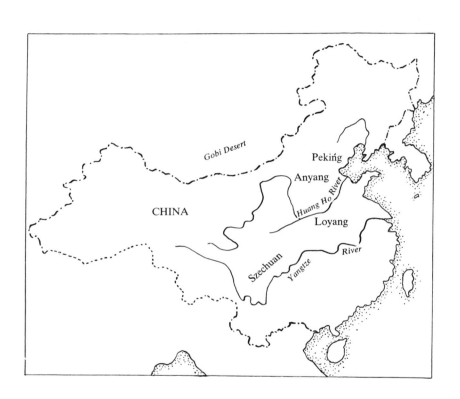

Gobi Desert

CHINA

Peking

Anyang

Huang Ho River

Loyang

Szechuan

Yangtze River

PART ONE

CHINA

The heart of the Far East is China, for China was the first land there to develop civilization. From Chinese civilization came the inventions, the philosophy, the literature, the great men who made possible the growth of civilization in other Far Eastern lands. China's influence has also been felt far outside the Far East. When Marco Polo told of its wonders his countrymen could not believe him, for he was describing a civilization in many ways more advanced than that of medieval Italy. Scientists are only now beginning to find out how Chinese civilization came into being. The evidence is still scarce, but what there is describes a fascinating story.

1

CHINESE BEGINNINGS

China is a diverse land. Its many thousands of square miles include broad and narrow, fertile and infertile valleys, wide stretches of desert, seas of alluvial land, high mountains, rolling foothills, sharp canyons, wind-ridden plateaus, mighty rivers, tiny streams, and a coast both low and rugged. In ancient times much of China was forest-covered or dark with wild grasses where roamed deer, elk, elephant, and tiger. Where the monsoon winds reach the land on the south the climate is tropical; where the north winds blow out of Siberia across the Gobi Desert the climate can be bitter cold in winter yet delightful in summer. In between, in keeping with its land diversity, China has all kinds of climatic zoning—"micro-zones," one calls them.

The geographical diversity is matched by the diversity of China's people. At least five thousand years ago the prehistoric people of the region we now call China were settled in or were settling into many of the microzones. There were fishers, hunters, gatherers; people who found the game of the forest conducive to their way of life as against those who lived in the grassy regions of otherwise desert country or those who gained substantial subsistence on the shores of lakes and rivers. All of these people knew very well indeed the advantages and disadvantages of the place where they lived. Where there were wild forms of plants such as millet and rape and perhaps rice there is little doubt that the people had some recognition of the nutritional value of even the wild forms. Whether this led to the kinds of experimentation that would result in agriculture is something we don't yet know, any more than we know that these early prehistoric people's knowledge of clay, native metal, and hard stone led to the innovations of pottery making, metal smelting, and jade carving. Until recently some scientists have thought that many things such as agriculture and bronze-casting came to the Chinese region from the West, but more thoughtful scholars today, seeing the new archaeological discoveries in China and knowing more about the native genius of prehistoric peoples, are not at all sure that these important advances were not made in-

Bronze bears, Han Dynasty

digenously. The proof is still to come. In the following pages some ideas about this are set down; they may be all wrong. That is the marvel of archaeology: the next turn of the spade may reveal a secret long hidden by time.

It is certain, however, that Chinese civilization did not grow up in one place even though it might first appear there. What is clear is that no one people or region made all the steps that led to civilization themselves. Each region made its own contribution, until at last on the north China plain all the contributions were brought together, and urban life, which is the true marker of civilization, emerged. What brought all these contribution together? That, too, eludes us, but again some ideas are suggested in the following pages.

2

THE FIRST FARMERS
ON THE YELLOW RIVER

The Chinese were among the ancient world's greatest historians. For almost three thousand years records have been kept by the Chinese of the events that occurred as one emperor after another succeeded to the throne in an almost endless row. From the time these records started, one thing was always noted by the writers: the proper times for planting and harvesting. But the Chinese were already tilling their fields perhaps two thousand years before writing was even known in eastern Asia.

It is thought by some that the Chinese may have first learned how to farm when the early villagers of Iran settled in Central Asia. The Chinese were probably seminomadic hunters, herders, and fishers at that time, but some undoubtedly were experimenting with the wild plants which eventually they would cultivate. Perhaps the Chinese developed agriculture independently.

The land of China is fruitful. In mountainous western

China there are wide, fertile valleys. The rivers flow eastward to join the greatest river of the East, the mighty Huang Ho (or Yellow River), which flows through a great flat plain. This plain became the homeland of the Chinese, the place where more people would live than in any other region of the earth.

Westward of modern China's capital, Peking, there is a line of hills rising one beyond the other. These mark the boundary of the plateau in Inner Asia at whose heart are the arid wastes of the Gobi Desert. For hundreds of miles there is hardly a tree or stream of water—just open land of gravel, sand, and exposed strata of stone. Yet this barren region has played a significant role in building Chinese civilization.

The reason for the Gobi's importance lies in the nature of the climate of North China. In the summer the winds come over the mountains of the south, bringing some rain from the sea. But in the winter the cold winds of Inner Asia sweep over the Gobi, picking up fine particles of earth and carrying them in great dusty clouds to the Chinese plain, where the dust is deposited. This process has been going on for thousands of years, resulting in the building up of a vast plain of dust (loess) seasonally refertilized by its Gobi parent. This dust region is one of the most fertile in the world. Properly used, its crops of wheat, barley, and millet are rich and abundant.

It was to the proper and understanding use of this land that the early Chinese farmers were dedicated.

3

ON THE SHORES
OF THE CHINA SEA

One of the great mysteries of the study of the past is that of the origin of Chinese civilization. Much as the Chinese themselves like to claim their independent origins, what is known of China's birth evidences her early borrowing from many peoples and cultures. It has been mentioned that agriculture possibly came from the west, from Iran, and there were other things of possible western origin too: pottery-making, metallurgy, brick-building, wheeled vehicles, and perhaps the idea of writing. There was another region which also contributed.

China has a very long, irregular coast facing to the east on the China Sea. Here for centuries fishermen have lived off the abundant sea life that flourishes in the warm water. Some actually have homes on the water, spending the greater part of their lives afloat. Since it appears almost certain that the Chinese originally came from North Asia and were landsmen, when did some of them take to the sea? Was there anyone there before them? Archaeologists have been exploring those almost unknown coasts for answers to this mystery.

Whoever the ancient people were who lived on the seacoast, they were important to the beginnings of China's civilization. To the north the Chinese coast reached Korea, and beyond Korea to Siberia or Japan. From the people of the north came useful objects, such as textured pottery, bone needles, polished stone objects, varieties of knives, perhaps even drums and religious dancing.

One theory has it that while the people of the North China plain were cultivating the soil, the people of the coast were probably moving farther and farther to the south, developing the techniques of fishing. Perhaps they learned of the advantages of the stable outrigger canoe from fishing peoples on the coast of Indo-China. The ability to sail freely over the sea in search of fish has always been an economic advantage of great importance, and the demand for good sailing craft is a very old one. When these men had boats they must have sailed to many places: the isles of Indonesia, the Philippines, and Formosa. They brought with them the things they had learned along the coast of China. In this way many of the cultures of the eastern seas may have got their start.

It is known that not all of these fishermen lived by the sea. Some found fresh-water fish more palatable and lived along the rivers. These men probably brought the cultures of the coast inland. Inland were the prehistoric hunters, herders, gatherers, and farmers, all living in their own ways, All these ways of life would be blended eventually into Chinese civilization.

4

A CHINESE VILLAGE

The early Chinese farmers (?–1800 B.C.) lived in villages situated in the midst of their fields. Chinese villages were usually quite large, sometimes several acres in extent. The houses were sometimes circular and sometimes square. In the latter case the house was frequently sunk into the ground, which meant one had to step down in order to enter.

The walls of these houses were made of wattle and daub. That means that they were screens of branches or reeds covered with mud-clay. About the room were wooden posts sunk into the floor; these supported the thatched roof. The floors were made of pounded earth—practically the first thing a villager did on building a house was to pound the floor into hardness by tamping the clay with wooden pounders. In the center of the room was a fire pit or an oven, so there must have been a smokehole in the roof.

Outside the houses archaeologists have uncovered storage pits with traces of millet in them. Big stone hoes, large storage pots, and sickle knives have been found. Such

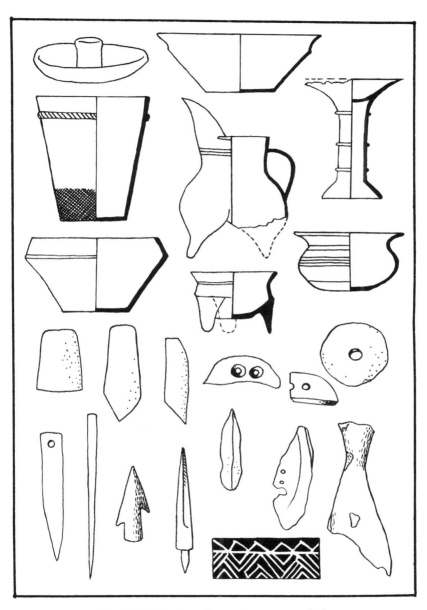

Neolithic tools and vessels, ca. 2000 B.C.

Painted pottery, ca. 2000 B.C.

Li tripod, ca. 2000 B.C.

objects are proof that these people were farmers. They also had pigs, sheep, and dogs in the village. Hooks and harpoons prove that the early Chinese fished, and sling pellets and arrowpoints indicate that they hunted to supplement their diet.

They wove a bast cloth and manufactured handsome pottery, some of which they painted with fluid geometric or animal designs.

Life most certainly centered on farming, and most of these early villages were probably self-centered, independent units for which change was indicated only by the seasons: when to plant, when to harvest, when to store. Not very much was known about the outside world, nor was there a real need to learn about it. Trade apparently played a very small part in earliest China, and people were perhaps too busy earning their livelihood to wander over the countryside. The individual's world was usually bounded by the lands of neighboring villages. Far travel was to be avoided. The nearer one was to one's fields and house the better. It was this strong attachment to home that formed the basis of Chinese character and society long before China became a nation.

5

"FIELDS, GARDENS, HOUSES, GRAVES"

To write about China is to write about the soil, for no people on the earth has been more devoted to the land than the Chinese. Families live in the midst of fields that they have cultivated for many centuries. These fields never lose their fertility because the Chinese have known that where crops are grown something is removed from the soil. That "something" which nourishes the plants and makes them fruitful has to be replaced. Annually, as a part of their duty to the land, the soil is refertilized. What has been taken is replaced. The Chinese have been doing this for so long that it could well be that they were the first people of the world to realize how man could replenish the soil regularly by fertilizing.

The idea that each generation is responsible for the maintenance of the fertility of the land it has inherited, so that it may pass that land on to a new generation in the same condition as it has been received, is a very important part of the Chinese concept that one's duty in life is to respect the past and to prepare for the future.

18

"Dancing" cranes, tomb tile, Han Dynasty

There is an ancient saying, *"t'ien, yuan, lu, mo,"* which means "fields, gardens, houses, graves." Altogether, the expression signifies "home." The Chinese peasant looking from his home sees the surrounding fields and knows that those fields grow the crops which nourish his family and mark his wealth; he observes the little garden near his house where are grown the vegetables that flavor his diet; he sees the houses and fields of his family, of his neighbors, and the halls where the tablets of the ancestors are kept; the graves on the hillside are those of the past generations whose labor made possible the "fields, gardens, and houses" of the present. To the Chinese the qualities *"t'ien, yuan, lu, mo"* must each be present if his home is truly his home.

Many Chinese stories told of how sad it was to leave home and how happy it was to return. The Chinese felt that home was like the root in the ground that made possible the growth of a tree. No man could be full-grown without his

"Red bird," stone relief, Han Dynasty

roots in his home. The wanderer and the soldier were pitied because the vital root of "home" had been cut off. The Chinese thought that this was one reason why soldiers and wanderers were frequently evil and causers of crime. They had no home roots and thus there was nothing to nourish them to mature responsible life.

If one understands the real meaning of *"t'ien, yuan, lu, mo,"* one understands a very important quality of Chinese life. The Chinese have respected this concept for many centuries. We don't know when it actually began, but certainly the idea of home and land being one and the same was conceived before China achieved civilization. The same thing is true of another characteristic Chinese idea—the reverence for ancestors.

6

THE SPIRIT
OF THE ANCESTORS

Though archaeology can only describe aspects of the material life of ancient China, traditions have survived into history, and these add to the re-creation of life in the past. "Ancestor worship" is one of these traditions.

To the ancient Chinese the world was filled with spirits. These were manifestations of a mysterious living force that permeated all things. These spirits might be found in a mountain, a tree, or an animal, or yet in a rock, a twig, or an eye. This spirit world could drastically affect one's life by bringing fortune or misfortune as one strived to achieve goals of one kind or another, like sowing grain, or building a wall, or bringing a load of wood home. Amulets, spells, prayers, incantations, and special rites were used to set the average farmer in balance with these forces.

There were some spirits that required very special attention, those of the ancestors, and they have retained special place in the life of the traditional Chinese even today.

Bronze masks, Shang Dynasty

According to Chinese belief, the family is not simply the living group of father, mother, sons, daughters, uncles, aunts, cousins, and grandparents; it also includes the dead relatives, both those newly deceased and the many generations of the past. More than this, the unnamed individuals of the future have to be considered as an integral part of the familial chain that links past, present, and future. The living individual then stands in an important relationship to this large family. His survival, his daily acts, the character of his life, can directly affect the well-being of the family. He thus has to exercise care in whatever he does for the good of everyone concerned. But he is not in complete control of the situation, for the ancestors have wills of their own.

When a man dies he becomes a spirit, and his spirit must be treated properly by his living relatives. If this is done, the ancestor spirit helps in bringing good fortune; if not, bad luck may come.

Prayers to the departed, offerings of food and drink, even sacrifices, were means of appeasing the ancestor spirits. Sometimes when an important task was to be done, the living might request the dead to tell them whether they stood a good chance to complete the work. In ancient times this was done through scapulamancy—a process in which the scapula bone of an animal was heated over a fire and the resulting cracks in the overheated bone were interpreted. Sometimes the request was written on the bone, and because of this, examples of China's oldest known writing have survived. This writing is known as oracle writing.

Of course, not all the spirits were those of the ancestors. The spirits of the earth and sky were also very important, and many were the offerings and the sacrifices to these important deities—even human beings were sacrificed

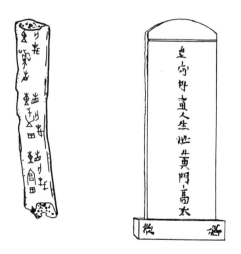

Scapula with "oracle" writing, Shang Dynasty (left); ancestor tablet, wood, nineteenth century A.D.(right)

as the ancient Chinese sought to maintain the fertility of the soil and to appease the wrath of the supernatural world.

The ancestor cult was the most important part of Chinese worship because it was the most personal. Later this cult was extended to the emperor of China as the father of his people and as the godlike "Son of Heaven." Ancestors of emperors were worshiped in the same way as one's own ancestors, particularly in the imperial courts. The cult of the ancestor emperors played a very important part in holding China together through many centuries of her existence.

China had emperor rulers for over three thousand years. The last one was deposed in 1912. Emperors gave their name to a period and their family name to a dynasty. A dynasty was defined as a family line of rulers, and this was one reason the Chinese people gave their loyalty to various dynasties, for the imperial family was regarded as an ideal of what a family ought to be. When that family no longer represented that ideal, the Chinese people could and sometimes did overthrow the dynasty. In fact the history of China has often been told in terms of the rise and fall of imperial dynasties.

7

THE CITY
OF THE SHANG

As the Chinese trace their history, the earliest dynasty was called the Hsia. This dynasty is partly legend, partly fact, but archaeologists have found no trace of the Hsia people or their cities and towns. The next dynasty was called the Shang, and its rulers controlled North China. That too was a lost dynasty until quite recently.

Around 1900 several high officials at the court of Peking discovered that the writing on certain bones brought into the city for sale by peasants was quite primitive and unusual. This, of course, was the oracle writing. Magnificent bronzes of very fine workmanship were also appearing in the bazaar. These objects whetted the desire of the officials to locate the place where they were coming from. But the peasants, anxious to preserve their source of new income, were uncooperative.

Some years passed, and several Occidentals and Chinese finally located the place. It was in the midst of the great

Detail of a bronze vessel, Shang Dynasty

North China plain in a bend of the Huan River, a branch of the Huang Ho near Anyang. In spite of bandits and armed peasants, the investigators excavated in the shapeless mounds and revealed the great city of Yin, capital of the Shang Dynasty.

The Shangs had chosen their capital site well, for the water of the river surrounded it on three sides, protecting it as effectively as a moat. It appears certain that the remaining (southern) side of the city was protected by a wall.

There is every indication that the Chinese were by now (c. 1300 B.C.) attaining a civilized status, for the appearance of cities marks the appearance of civilization. Yin seems to fill all the requirements of a city: large buildings, elaborate social organization, specialists, large population, and kings and courts.

The city was divided into sections, each with its own group of special craftsmen. One district was the place of the bronze-workers. Archaeologists digging there found heaps of

Bronze wine cup with swallow cover, Shang Dynasty

ashes and slag, by-products of the manufacture of bronze. Occasionally they found the broken molds in which bronze vessels, weapons, or ornaments were cast. In another district bone was carved into hairpins, spoons, arrowheads, ladles, and the like; elsewhere a profusion of stone knives, spears, bowls, utensils, and ornaments were sure signs of stone workers. Fragments of jade proved that that classic Chinese stone was appreciated at least thirteen hundred years before Christ.

In another quarter of the city were the remains of large buildings, the royal palaces and public buildings. When the archaeologists dug these clear they discovered great rectangular platforms made of pounded earth. In these platforms were holes in rows, which obviously were used to hold the bases of pillars, but they gave very little idea as to what the upper part of the buildings was like. However, someone

Reconstruction of a Shang Dynasty house

studying the signs on the oracle bones discovered that the symbol for a building was 俎 . This was really a picture of one end of a structure, the lower part of the sign being the earthen platform. The building had post holes up the middle of the platform, which held the pillars that supported the peak of the roof shown in the sign.

Some of these buildings must have been built on a grand scale. One measured 92 feet long by 26 feet wide. The

Bear's head, stone, Shang Dynasty

posts and the beam ends that protrude were probably elaborately carved with figures of animals and humans, and stone or bronze sculptures were set into the wood as decorative elements. The walls between the pillars were of wood or brick plastered over and painted in polychrome designs of various kinds. Entrance into the building was from one of the long sides up a small stairway into a hall. Torchlight reflected the splendor of the interior—a shadowy vision of bright colors, shining metal, and soft wood—certainly a suitable setting for an audience with an imperial prince.

Jade rabbit, ornament, Shang Dynasty

Near these buildings were found pits in which the Shangs stored their valuable articles. In one place almost six thousand objects were uncovered, including some of jade, gold, and bronze. Cowrie shells were found in great abundance in these pits. These shells had to be brought hundreds of miles from the southern coasts of China. They were valuable not only as scarce objects handsome to look upon, but as a kind of money for which things might be exchanged. The shells were frequently pierced and strung into necklaces, and one idea has it that the owner paraded his wealth, if he so chose, by wearing these necklaces in public.

Though so little is really known about the old Shang Dynasty, archaeology has given some idea of the true splendor of their city, the first Chinese capital.

8

KING AND CAPTIVE

The Shang king had died and joined his ancestors. His resting place was about to receive the royal body. Borne on a litter and preceded by his chariot, the body of the king was carried out of the city. A hundred prisoners marched behind the procession, dressed in ceremonial robes, and crowds of mourners burning incense and crying lamentations gathered all about.

The tomb was a deep square pit entered by means of a ramp at one end and a flight of stairs at the other. The interior of the tomb was lined with painted and carved wooden walls, and at its center the body of the king wrapped in his silk robes was placed. Servants brought his belongings and treasures to accompany him in his afterlife. The finest things that craftsmen could make were laid in the tomb: magnificent bronze vessels with monster faces and delicate tracery as decoration; pure white but elaborately decorated pottery vases; fine bronze helmets, spears, and axes; swathes of the finest silk; a musical stone that gave forth a rich note when

Bronze vessel, Shang Dynasty

struck; jade, turquoise, and gold ornaments; marble sculptures of frogs, cats, and monsters.

When this was done the chariot horses pulled the bronze-fitted chariot into the chamber and with it the charioteer, loyal retainer of his master, the king. The spoked wheels turned for the last time in this world, and then all was ready. As the priests chanted, several soldiers took their places at the foot of the ramp as eternal sentries guarding the tomb. Others killed the horses with quick blows. The charioteer quickly died from poison and was arranged in his proper place in the chariot. Gangs of men moved forward, some to shovel earth into the chamber while others tamped it down hard. From time to time some of the waiting prisoners of war were led forward; soldiers lopped their heads off with sudden blows of their axes. The heads were thrown into the tomb, where they were pounded down by the stamp-

Jade disk, fifth to third century B.C.

ing laborers; the bodies were hauled into separate graves. As the tomb fill rose higher, more of the prisoners were sacrificed, until with the last one the tomb was level with the surrounding soil and the dead were all gone. Sacrificial fires burned over the place, tended by the priests. The populace returned to the city, aware of a new spirit in their midst whom they must not forget in their daily prayers and rituals.

This account of the Shang royal tomb is based upon a series of archaeological discoveries. Unfortunately many of the tombs had been robbed of their principal treasures of bronze and gold, but by careful, painstaking work the archaeologists managed to reconstruct many things. Though the wood of the chariot had long since disappeared, the imprint of the wheel in the surrounding soil remained; by casting that imprint in plaster the wheel was then recovered, and a reconstruction of the original chariot made possible. By such methods much has been preserved that might otherwise be lost.

One might ask why so many people were sacrificed. It may have been because the king needed retainers in the other world. It may have been because the sacrifice of so many captives indicated the power of the king on earth.

9

CHARIOTS AND
THE END OF SHANG

Shang princes must have been dashing individuals. All their lives they were required to train, compete, and excel in such vigorous pursuits as hunting, archery, chariotry, and soldiering. They owed undying loyalty to the throne, which probably had a sacred character about it. Their loyalty was best expressed by accomplishments on its behalf. Prestige had a great deal to do with proof of manhood.

Archery contests, common in later China, seem to have been popular as early as the Shang period. The compound bow with its advantages to the horseman was a favorite weapon, and accuracy with it was continually sought.

In time of war the Shang princes mustered chariots for combat and supported these mobile units with foot soldiers. Each chariot carried a charioteer, a spearman (or axman), and an archer (usually a noble). Riding into combat at full speed over the open plain, these chariot units could either smash through their opponents or worry their flanks, where the accurate archery of the bowmen would cause great destruction. Mobility was the key to success in war, and this was achieved by archers shooting from moving chariots. In the role of warriors the Shang princes and nobles must have excelled, for the period probably lasted a good five hundred years. It was not until another chariot-using group of accurate archers produced more vigorous and perhaps less luxury-loving princes that the Shang lost control.

Pair of bronze horses, Shang Dynasty

10

THE CHOUS
AND CONFUCIUS

Ruling a kingdom in ancient China was a troublesome business. Communication was difficult, and knowledge of invasion by enemies often came too late for decisive action. The Shang rulers appear to have been at war continually with the peoples along their borders, particularly in the west. One group of these enemy peoples was called the Chou. Under their ruler, known only as "the Martial King," the Chous

Gilt bronze dragon head, late Chou Dynasty

Ritual bronze bell, late Chou Dynasty, ca. 600 B.C.

took advantage of Shang weaknesses and conquered them, thus founding the Chou Dynasty, which was to rule China for about eight hundred years. This period has been considered a golden age by most Chinese.

The Chous ruled over a number of feudal states, each of which was headed by a hereditary prince native to that state. The translators of the Chinese classics composed in this period regarded these state rulers in much the same way as dukes were regarded in medieval and Renaissance Europe. These men and their courts grew very powerful and in time brought about the collapse of the Chou Dynasty. They gained fame as patrons of art and learning. At their courts gathered ancient China's sage men, some of whom attained world fame for their wisdom. Among these great men were Lao-Tzu, Mencius, Mo-Tzu, and, the most famous of all, Confucius.

White jade tiger, Chou Dynasty

Confucius was born around 550 B.C. at a time when the rule of the Chous was weak and that of the dukes strong. Confucius was therefore born into a world of difficulties, for the dukes warred among themselves and in many of the states oppressed the people. As a young man he spent a great deal of time thinking about men's troubles and how they could be solved. He developed some specific ideas about these problems. He believed that peace and orderly living came from the proper fulfilment of one's role in life. This role was determined by one's relation to others. There were five basic relationships, and, in each, one had to fulfill a certain part: ruler and subject—a subject had to be submissive to the authority of the ruler; husband and wife—a wife had to obey the authority of the husband; father and son—the authority of the father required the son's submissive obedience; elder and younger brother—in which the younger must recognize the authority of elder; and friend and friend, which involved the virtuous qualities of justice, love, understanding, and comradery.

These relationships required that each individual truly understand his various roles in society with their specific duties and manners. A ruler was to temper discipline with benevolence; a subject was expected to be submissive in a sincere and respectful way; and a son was to obey, respect, and love at the same time.

Confucius taught at a kind of school of his own founding where young men were able to hear his views on life. They became his disciples and carried his ideas into the world. Some were even of princely families.

Confucius

Confucius was not only an administrator and a philosopher; he was also well aware of the vast literary heritage
that China already had. He compiled many ancient works
into more concise form, including the so-called classics, and
he contributed sayings of his own, particularly in the
Analects, some of the most famous of which are:

> Virtue does not live alone, she must have
> neighbors.
> To be slow to speak, but prompt to act, is the
> desire of the superior man.
> The superior man is exacting of himself; the
> common man is exacting of others.
> In serving your prince, make your service the
> serious concern, and let salary be a secondary matter.
> None can be a superior man who does not
> recognize the decrees of heaven.

Confucius believed that if a ruler was a good and just
administrator, the people would also be virtuous, since he
considered human nature to be basically good. He had
his chance to prove his views when he was made prime minister to the ruler of Lu. His success was extraordinary, and the
state of Lu became both prosperous and happy. After a time
the neighboring ruler of Ch'i, jealous and fearful of Lu, sent
a train of entertainers—musicians, clowns, and beautiful
women—as a gift to the ruler of Lu, who, in accepting them,
began the betrayal of his wise minister. Confucius had
warned that as soon as personal pleasure became more important than the harmony and sound administration of the state,
then the right rule he had demonstrated would collapse. That
is exactly what happened. Confucius, heartbroken by the event,

Ceremonial bronze wine vessel with animal cover,
late Western Chou Dynasty

wandered through China, hoping that some other ruler would use him to put his own state aright. But though many listened to him and he had many loyal followers, he never was given another opportunity. He died at the age of seventy-two, still hoping that men would sincerely use the wisdom he had brought to them.

Pole end in the form of a dragon's head,
gilt bronze, late Chou Dynasty

11

THE TAO

Second only to Confucianism has been the religious philosophy of Taoism. It seems that at the time Confucius was roaming about North China, thinking and teaching, there also was living a philosopher named Lao-Tzu. Not very much is known about Lao-Tzu except that he wrote a short book or treatise, which is also called "the Lao-Tzu." Lao-Tzu himself is but a shadow—but an important shadow nonetheless. Out of his thinking and that of his followers in succeeding generations arose a profound and meaningful view of the world, which affected not only the arts but government itself.

The term *"Tao"* basically means "truth." Truth has two parts. The first part can be understood, such as the flight of a bird or the appearance of the sea; the things one sees, the things that are tangible. The second part is beyond understanding; it can neither be seen nor comprehended. It is what is called an ultimate principle or truth. For example, living things exist because one sees them, but why they exist or what existence really is is not known.

Taoist painting,
nineteenth century A.D.

The Taoist schools of Chinese painting exemplify this philosophy. Typically, Taoist paintings are landscapes with panoramas of cliffs, bodies of water, trees, clouds, and open fields. In these landscapes are tiny figures of men, animals, houses, and boats. These paintings were created by adherence to the conventions of calligraphy, so that every feature is clearly depicted. Yet there is a misty and a mystical quality about the scene—misty because the artist knew how nature veils part of every landscape in her own way, and mystical because many little scenes were created by the artist so that one can view the painting by the hour and still find more and more scenes within it.

Two things are apparent in a Taoist painting: how insignificant man and his creations are in the midst of nature; and how mountains, clouds, trees, rivers, rocks, and man blend together into one unity. That unity is, of course, Tao. Thus the result of all the complications, tangles, and disorders of the natural world is a unity that is harmonious and beautiful. Man who lives in the midst of that teeming world thinks he can bring order to nature by struggling and trying to change things. As long as he does that he suffers and brings pain to himself and to others. He gets nowhere, for he is not following the Tao. He does not perceive the order that lies beyond all things.

Taoists conceive of the universe as consisting of two principles, the active male principle called the *"yang"* and the passive female principle called the *"yin."* These two together form the perfect harmony, the Tao, from which all things come. These two principles must never be out of harmony or chaos results and the Tao is veiled.

To the ancient Taoists the best government was one

Yang and yin, Taoist symbol

which was hardly known to the people because affairs were in such order in accordance with the Tao that minimum rule was all that was necessary. For the individual a life of common sense, frugality, and humility was truly Taoist. As in the Christian belief, so the Taoist thought that the "meek would inherit the earth." Comparing weakness and humbleness to water, a favorite Taoist comparison, Lao-Tzu said:

> Of all things yielding and weak in the world,
> None is more so than water
> But for attacking what is unyielding and strong,
> Nothing is superior to it,
> Nothing can take its place.

In its emphasis on the power of non-aggression, on the beauties and harmonies of nature, and the falsity of so many of man's purposes, Taoism made a major contribution to Chinese art and thought.

Bronze cranes, late Chou Dynasty

Taoism, Confucianism, and other religious philosophies, as well as a whole spectrum of Chinese accomplishments, have come down to the modern world because of the extraordinary Chinese writing system. Because these things were written down they have survived, and thus it has been possible to come in contact with the words and thoughts of wise men centuries away from us.

12

CHINESE WRITING AND SPEECH

Chinese writing is the most expressive of all the world's writing systems. One can say things with Chinese characters that cannot be said with the twenty-six signs of the English alphabet. Chinese has over fifty thousand signs, which can be used in as many combinations as one might wish to express complicated ideas such as "imagination, dreams, virtue, and truth."

The Chinese spoken language has many dialects, but it is limited linguistically in number of sounds. For example, the Chinese have difficulty pronouncing the "r" sound of European languages, since "r" is not typically part of their language. All languages have sound limitations, but Chinese is more limited in this respect than others.

One word may have many meanings—the word *shih* has over sixty!—and to get around this problem the Chinese have evolved a system of tones. Four tones are generally used in North China, and there are as many as nine in the south.

47

The four main tones are:

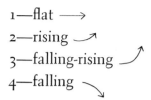

1—flat $\longrightarrow$
2—rising
3—falling-rising
4—falling

By using these different tones with a word like *shan,* different meanings are expressed:

shan[1]—a mountain
shan[2]—beautiful
shan[3]—to flash
shan[4]—a fan

But that is not all. The word *shan* in the four tones also has other meanings. In such cases the meaning and the accent of the sentence must be listened to carefully. The Chinese speak with rhythm, and this combined with the tones gives the spoken language the musical quality that makes it unmistakable.

The written language makes up for the problems of the spoken tongue by providing a different character or characters for each word or meaning. Most Chinese characters are made up of combinations of 214 signs called radicals. To look up a word in a Chinese dictionary, one must know which of these signs is its principal or key radical.

Scholars are generally agreed that picture writing was the start of Chinese writing, but there are no examples of this early form. The more advanced oracle writings provide the first clues as to how modern Chinese writing came into being. There are also clues in the modern writing itself.

Here are examples of Chinese characters:

人 —*jen*—a man

上 —*shang*— (a man above) means *above* or *on*

下 —*hsia*— (a man below) means *down* or *under*

日 —*jih*—means *day* or *sun*

月 —*yüeh*—means *moon*

明 —*ming*—means *splendid* or *bright*

In these last three words the ancient writings suggest that the sun sign was derived from ⊙ and the moon from ☽. Sun and moon together of course mean bright. To find out what the sign 明 means in the dictionary, decide which of the two signs 日 or 月 is the main radical. If you decide wrong then you have to use the other character as the main radical. Then count the number of strokes in the other sign. Thus the main radical in *ming* is 日 and the number of strokes that make up 月 is four: ノ 𠃌 ² ⁻ ³ ⁻ ⁴ ⁻

To find the character, one looks in the dictionary under four-stroke radicals combined with a four-stroke sign.

The Chinese put a great deal of emphasis on and have great pride in calligraphy, which is the art of writing these characters. Traditionally a brush is used, and the strokes are worked out according to whether a line can be completed with one easy movement of the brush or not. The character *yung,* meaning "forever," is used by the Chinese as a guide to good calligraphy for it contains most of the kinds of strokes needed to form a character. The principle of stroke order is top to bottom and left to right.

The beauty with which calligraphers create these characters makes their writings prized not only for their content but for their art. That is why in the history of Chinese painting most artists are outstanding calligraphers and indeed bring a calligrapher's style to their works.

Some idea as to how Chinese characters originated can be gained from the list below. It gives an inkling as to the teeming thought, history, and wonder that lie behind Chinese writing, a writing that began before the Shang kings ruled North China.

Chinese	English	Oracle	Modern
li	To stand	大	立
niu	An ox	Ψ	牛
yang	A sheep	Ψ	羊

13

THE GREAT WALL

The feudal situation that dominated China in the Chou period appeared to many as a great weakness, particularly in view of the barbarian hordes in the north and west who continually raided the settled areas of North China. The Chinese states along these troubled borders were usually at war with the barbarians and had to maintain strong armies. They built walls along their frontiers to keep the mobile barbarians out, garrisoning them with a system of sentry towers and moving patrols.

One of these frontier states, that of Ch'in, became so powerful that in 318 B.C. the Ch'in ruler led his armies to conquer the rich province of Szechuan. This gave his successors a base for further conquests. In 234 B.C. one of these princes conquered the last of the Chou states and became China's first emperor, Shih-huang-ti.

Shih-huang-ti broke up the feudal states by dividing China into forty-one districts, each with its military and civil officials. These men all owed their allegiance directly to the

The Great Wall of China at Nankon

emperor. The districts were connected by tree-lined roads, canals were built, and rich areas south of the Yangtze River were added to the empire.

Because most literature had idealized the old Chinese way of life, he had many of the old books burned, punishing severely anyone who concealed one. He also connected the walls of the former frontier states so as to form one continuous wall on the whole northern border—a truly colossal feat. This was the basis of the Great Wall of world fame.

In spite of all Shih-huang-ti's efforts, almost as soon as he died there was a rebellion and the Ch'in Dynasty collapsed, to be replaced by the most famous and powerful of Chinese dynasties—that of the Han. This began a new life for the Chinese, who learned to call themselves "Men of Han."

Stylized bird, tomb tile, Han Dynasty

14

THE MIGHTY HAN

At the time the Romans were beginning the conquest of the Mediterranean world, which eventually would result in the creation of one of the greatest empires in history, China was creating its own imperial world. Shih-huang-ti had left China in very bad condition. Feudal armies marched everywhere, looting and burning, while out of Inner Asia came raiding barbarian armies. No one group was powerful enough to reunite the states until a young officer named Liu of the House of Han appeared. Liu was an energetic man. He used Confucian ideas to reorganize the government at home and fought savage wars with the barbarians from beyond the Great Wall. The most important of these barbarian peoples were the Hsiung-Nu. On one raid they almost captured Liu. It was not until the reign of the Emperor Wu, one of Liu's successors, that the Chinese were able to attack and beat the Hsiung-Nu in their own territory.

Emperor Wu was surrounded by gifted men, among them a number of excellent soldiers. With their help the

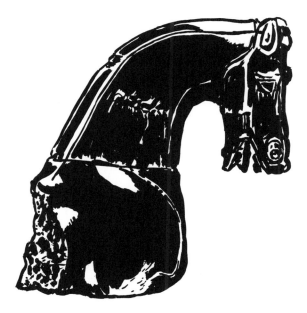

Jade carving of a horse, Han Dynasty

Han emperor was able to conquer parts of Korea and the far south of China beyond the Yangtze, the great river that marks the boundary between North and South China. Most remarkable of all was the movement of Chinese armies across the difficult desert roads of Inner Asia to the gates of western Central Asia. Here, inspired by the fine horses and the mineral wealth, and to control the passes across which went the commerce between east and west, the Han Dynasty established military control. Here Chinese soldiers later fought Roman legionnaires when the two great empires' interests clashed for a short time.

A great deal is known about the Han Dynasty, for archaeologists have for many years been digging up evidence of their arts and crafts, palaces and tombs. The people of Han

Tomb relief, Han Dynasty

had paper, developed an excellent calendar, established libraries, created a dictionary, recorded sunspots, timed eclipses, did master work in jade-carving, lacquering, ceramics, painted and carved fine art; they brought new plants from the west, such as the grapevine, and introduced advanced methods of farming, which involved especially the development of rice cultivation in South China.

It was in the Han period too that historians appeared who studied the wealth of documents that had survived from the past or were part of the record of their time. Out of their studies grew several famous histories—histories that are the first of a line of histories up to the present, for which China is justly famous.

It was a cosmopolitan age, and in the imperial cities it was not unusual to see Koreans, Central Asians, Persians, Tibetans, and peoples of the Indian Ocean regions. These were usually envoys, merchants, scholars, or craftsmen. The wares of foreign lands—iron, wool, wine, furs—were exchanged for Chinese lacquer, jade, and silk. So desirous were Romans to obtain silk that the Emperor Tiberius, who reigned at the time of Christ, had to pass an edict forbidding the use of silk as dress in order to prevent the flow of gold toward China.

One of the greatest accomplishments of the Han period was the establishment of Confucian scholars as the leaders in government under the monarchy. Previously the most important posts were held by members of the aristocracy. Since the ideas of Confucius were accepted as the best means of running the government, it was important that Confucian thinkers hold the positions of responsibility. These thinkers believed that the world was divided into three parts,

Dragon and warrior, tomb tile, Han Dynasty

each with its own function and responsibilities: heaven, from whence came light and rain and which was the place of the spirit; earth, which provided for water, agriculture, and other such qualities; and man and his government. These functioned in harmony as long as each carried out its special responsibilities. It was unthinkable that heaven and earth would not do so. Only man failed in his government and thus promoted discord.

The solution lay in observing the rules and the rites taught by Confucius as he himself had handed them down from times more ancient. The knowledge that men had obtained of heaven through astronomy and of earth through economics were to be applied to government. The study of government was considered as suitable a study for a scholar as was the study of the stars.

Colleges where the Confucian classics could be taught were set up. By a system of examinations in these subjects, a student could qualify as an official of the government. Gradually there spread throughout China a kind of civil service based on Confucian principles. This acted for the government so successfully that the Han period became celebrated for its maintenance of benign and orderly administration.

The government system begun in Han times was to prevail in China for centuries. In time it was to give the

Painted clay model of a house, Han Dynasty

Chinese a governmental system that reached from the individual family to the emperor himself. This system did not fail China until Western civilization with its dynamic advances in science and technology eroded the basis of Confucianism.

The Han Dynasty fell when the military part of the government took advantage of the weak character of some of the later Han emperors and, by plots and civil troubles, broke the power of the Han government. The farmers of China, made miserable by the military leaders, revolted and overthrew the House of Han.

In the last century or so of Han rule Buddhism had been spreading among the Chinese, who had first come in contact with it in the western part of their empire. Its quiet, moderate philosophy was not too different from many basic ideas of Taoism and Confucianism, so it quickly gained favor in China. Its arrival was part of a new era for that land, and it marked the end of ancient China.

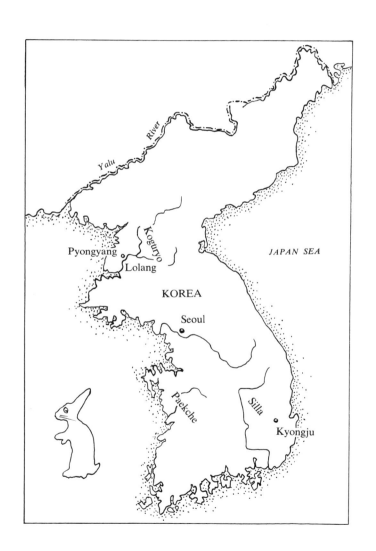

Yalu River

Koguryo

Pyongyang
Lolang

JAPAN SEA

KOREA

Seoul

Paekche

Silla

Kyongju

PART TWO

KOREA

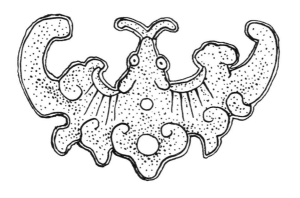

Generally northwest of China is the peninsula of Korea, a land that has known Chinese conquest but has come down to the modern world in possession of a unique culture. Long closed to the West, it has sometimes been called the "Hermit" kingdom because of its isolation. Actually, far from being "hermitlike," Korea has played a vital role in the Far East as the bridge between China and Japan. A knowledge of Korea is important in understanding how varied are the peoples of the Far East.

15

KOREA—"RABBITLAND"

Some Koreans traditionally compare their land to a rabbit because on a map Korea does look like the side view of a rabbit! The eastern side of the peninsula is the backbone of the rabbit; the long extension stretching northward on the Sea of Japan to Manchuria is its ear, while the various protuberances on the western, or Yellow Sea, side make an excellent nose and charming paws. There is also a bit of a tail facing on the Strait of Tsushima, the body of water that separates Korea from Japan.

Korea is a mountainous country with many valleys. The best farming land is along the western coast and in the south, where the land is flatter and less rocky. It is in this region that most Koreans live.

Korea has a temperate climate—four seasons in the year with hot summers and cold winters. However, because the land is so mountainous, local climate can vary from region to region. The south can have an almost tropical climate while way up north where there are high mountains and coniferous forests the climate may be very cold.

As early as the time the Chinese were first settling the lands of the Yellow River, tribes from Siberia and Manchuria were moving into Korea. Some of these were probably associated with the seacoast people mentioned as important in early China. These people would seem to have been hunters and fishers and perhaps herdsmen. Yet they also settled on the land and began to till it, probably sometime after agriculture was being practiced in China. Archaeology has not yet revealed that story.

There is a Korean legend that tells about the son of the creator of the universe, named Hwanung. Hwanung decided to come down from heaven and live on earth as a man. Traditionally, he made his descent, along with a host of spirits as his retinue, in the year 2333 B.C.

Hwanung made his home on a mountaintop, and he was quite content. Then one day a bear came and asked about the secrets of heaven. Hwanung told the bear to eat certain plants and stay in a cave for a while. The bear did so, and at the end of the time was turned into a beautiful woman. Soon afterward she gave birth to a fine son, named Tangun. Tangun was so handsome and manly that when one day some tribesmen found him they made him their king. Tangun was thus the first king of Korea. That is why the Korean calendar starts in the year 2333 B.C.

Tangun was a great king who taught his people agriculture and the arts of settled life and thus laid the basis for Korean civilization. His miraculous birth and his relationship to the great creator god have led the Koreans to believe in one great god as the ruler of the world. In Eastern Asia the

Korean stone tools, ca. 400 A.D.

bear was often used as a symbol of tribes and their beliefs. That it was through the transformation of the bear by divine will that settled life was brought to Korea suggests that the legend was based on the actual historical conversion from nomadic life to settled life.

Another story with a better basis in history tells of the Chinese wise man Kija who left China with his followers about the time the Shang Dynasty was falling. Kija settled among the tribes in northwestern Korea. He built a settlement where the modern North Korean city of Pyongyang now stands.

Kija brought to Korea the knowledge of China: how to take care of bullocks and pigs, how to irrigate crops, how to make silk, and the techniques of pottery-making and bronze-casting. Best of all, he created just laws and made them apply to government and people alike. A wise and good man, much loved by the Koreans, Kija has often been referred to as the builder of Korean civilization.

Korea gained much from its geographical position on the seas. The Koreans were excellent fishermen, and they were the sailors of Eastern Asia. Their boats plied the high seas between Japan and China and stopped at the numerous islands that dot the coasts. This helped to make Korean culture international, though it remained unique in many ways.

The story of Kija is an indication of how important Chinese culture has been to Korea. Yet it is to Central Asia that the Korean people owe their origins. Their language belongs to the Central Asian language family called Ural-Altaic, which includes such tongues as Mongolian and Turkish. Japanese too belongs to this group. The Korean written language is entirely different from Chinese in that it is based on an alphabet called Hangul.

In appearance Koreans are like the Japanese and Chinese; that is, they belong to the Mongoloid racial stock, which like the Caucasoid or white race has many different branches.

Not very much is known of Korean life before the first existing records, which appeared in the time of the Han Dynasty of China. One thing is certain, however, and that is that the old religion of Central Asia was not forgotten, though it was modified by settled life. This religion has been called "animistic" because it had as its central theme the idea that the world was full of spirits. As in Chinese "ancestor worship," which probably also derived from ancient animistic ideas, these spirits could be good or bad. One had to be careful with the spirit world for it could be good or bad according to one's actions. Indeed, a bad spirit could steal a good man's soul from his body and then jump into that

Korean Confucian scholars at the Confucian Temple, Seoul

body. Once this happened, the body might sicken or do evil things. To offset such events there were shamans or sorcerers and sorceresses who devised by magic ways of curing, placating evil spirits, and helping a person steer clear of trouble with the spirit world. Even today there are sorceresses in the countryside who help the farmers overcome bad luck.

Confucianism and Buddhism are now important religious beliefs in Korea, but each has its own Korean interpretation. This is important to note for Korea has always been vulnerable to the influences of powerful nations and yet has emerged uniquely itself.

During the Han Dynasty in the reign of Emperor Wu, a Chinese colony was created near where Kija had placed his settlement according to the tradition. Archaeologists working on the site of this ancient colony discovered that it really had been a prosperous city called Lolang with a population of over 400,000 people. Out of the tombs of Lolang has come an incredible treasure of arts and crafts, including lacquer boxes and bronze mirrors of magnificent workmanship. Through Lolang the culture of the Han Dynasty was brought to Korea. From that time on, Korea often reflected the civilization of China.

16

THE THREE KINGDOMS

Korea, because of its geography, has always had difficulty maintaining its unity as a nation. In the time of the colony of Lolang, there were three large kingdoms and many small ones in the land. The period was called that of the Three Kingdoms. Each kingdom had its roots in the various tribes that had come to Korea, some newly arrived and some from long ago.

The Koguryo kingdom had its seat in Northern Korea along the great Yalu River, which separates Korea from Manchuria in places. Being so close to Lolang, the Koguryo were much influenced by Chinese culture. Koguryo was also close to China and thus subject to the ambitions of various Chinese emperors. Wars with China occurred frequently. Koguryo also had to repel invasions by tribes from Manchuria. It was therefore a warlike state struggling to survive but richly adorned with the culture of China.

Paekche was a small state of Central Korea located in the area where the modern capital of South Korea, Seoul, now stands. Though small and really unwarlike, Paekche also received much of the civilization of China. Its cultural achievements were so great and its splendors so renowned that many peoples came to settle there or to admire and move on. Even objects from far distant Persia have been found in its archaeological remains. The sailors of Paekche moved about the Yellow Sea and brought Paekche artists to Japan. The Japanese were becoming interested in the civilization of China, and it was Paekche that brought much of that civilization to Japan. Paekche's cultural success aroused the envy of China and of other Korean states. Together these enemies crushed Paekche. The artists and men of learning fled to Japan. Their skills helped the Japanese to achieve a high degree of civilization.

One of the Korean states involved in the fall of Paekche was the powerful kingdom of Silla. Silla occupied most of Southern Korea, and with the help of China during the Tang Dynasty (A.D. 609) managed eventually even to conquer Koguryo. This brought practically all of Korea under one rule. Though the rulers of Silla said they were vassals of China, Korea was really quite independent.

The rule of Silla saw the fullest development of Korean civilization. The capital city, Kyongju, had over a million inhabitants, and it was so wealthy and splendid that even Moslems from the Middle East crossed Asia to visit and to trade and to see for themselves. The arts and crafts were highly developed. Under Chinese influence, good government prevailed and Buddhism was accepted. Rice cultivation, which was successful in the climate of Southern Korea, kept everyone well fed. Silla seemed destined to last a long time, but Japanese pirates, invasions by the tribes of the

Korean farmyard

north, and weak rulers eventually brought an end to Silla and to the period of the Three Kingdoms.

The next period, that of the Koryo Dynasty, does not belong to the ancient age. "*Koryo*" means "land of high mountains and sparkling streams," and this term has come down to us as "Korea." Actually the Koreans call their land Chosen, "land of the morning calm."

Korea played an important role in the cultural history of the Far East by helping to transmit the civilization of China to Japan. At the same time it created its own form of civilization. Like the rabbit which the shape of the land emulates, Korea has always had to be on the alert for danger but at the same time it has been good to look upon.

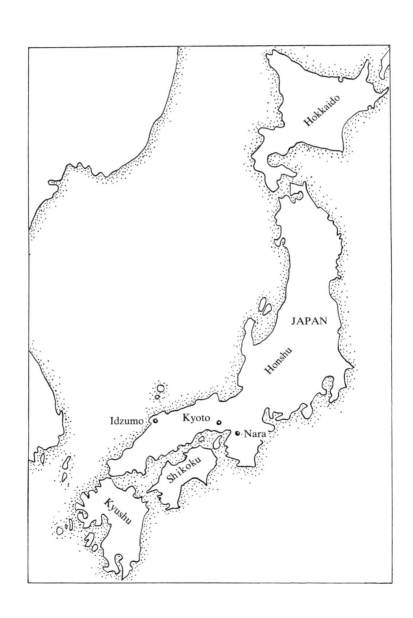

Hokkaido

JAPAN

Honshu

Idzumo Kyoto
Nara

Shikoku

Kyushu

PART THREE

JAPAN

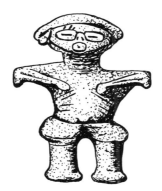

Japan is easternmost Asia. It is the farthest east of the Far Eastern lands; beyond are the broad reaches of the mighty Pacific Ocean. Though the Japanese are islanders, their view has been toward the land and not to the sea. As lovers of the land they have rivaled the Chinese, and their celebration of that love has created one of the supreme examples of human expression in the world, that of Japanese art. Like the Chinese, too, Japanese civilization is rooted in a hybrid past. How it created its own civilization out of that past is one of the stories archaeologists are trying very hard to tell.

17

EARLIEST JAPAN

The islands of Japan swing in a kind of half-moon shape just off the eastern coast of Asia. To the north the island of Sakhalin almost touches the coast of Siberia. On the southwest the narrow straits between Japan and Korea are dotted with "steppingstone" islands. Thus Japan, though clearly separated from the mainland by water, is also near enough to be readily accessible to mainlanders who want to get there.

And quite a few ancient peoples were anxious to cross the water and to settle in the mountainous country of Japan. Perhaps this was because the warm currents that flow northward out of the South China Sea and surround Japan support some of the most abundant fishing grounds of the world. Game too was plentiful on the forested slopes of this isolated land. Later when farmers came into the country they found rich fertile soil in pockets and plains in the valleys and in the foothills of the mountains. It may well have been that in remote times the isolated situation of Japan made it a refuge for harried peoples of the Asian continent.

In any case the earliest culture about which there is detailed evidence is called "Jomon" (cord-pattern), after its pottery decoration, which appears to have resulted from the impression of string or cords on the clay surface. This cord-pattern ware has also been found in Siberia and Korea. The bone and stone tools that have turned up along with the cord-pattern pottery are also of North Asian type, so that it seems clear that the Jomon culture is partly derived from North Asia.

On the island of Hokkaido, the northernmost of the main islands of Japan, there lives a group of people who are of a different race than the Japanese. They are heavy-boned, white-skinned, and have dark hair. They worship spirits of hunting and fishing and celebrate rites in a strange bear cult. They weave fine robes and decorate them with geometric designs of ancient origin. These people are the Ainu, and one theory has it that their ancestors were the bearers of the Jomon culture to Japan. Perhaps they originally lived in Siberia and migrated south across the straits into Japan, where they settled near the sea.

The ancient Jomon villages are frequently marked by enormous heaps of shells, proving that the old Jomon people were not fish-eaters alone but were well aware of the succulent properties of the clam and the oyster.

Japan in those days must have been an idyllic place. Fish and game were abundant, and there must have been considerable leisure time, which was unusual, for hunting people had to keep busy most of the time in order to live. Pottery work seems to have been one of the ways they used

Jomon figurines, pre-500 B.C.

their leisure time. Jomon potters shaped their bowls and jars in fantastic forms, including figurines of a very wonderful kind. Some of these are among the national treasures of Japan.

The Mongoloid people that invaded Japan and became the basic Japanese racial stock probably began to reach the islands from Korea during the later part of the Jomon period—sometime after 1000 B.C. They probably fought with the Ainu people and pushed them out of the south. At first they were hunters and fishers, but by 200 B.C. they had begun to use agriculture, especially rice cultivation. This was the basis for a stable economy and a new way of life.

This new period was called "Yayoi," and it was then that the truly Japanese character of society began to be formed. One important part of that character was the belief in the gods.

18

LEGENDARY BEGINNINGS

According to a story coming down from the past, in the beginning there was chaos out of which was formed hell and heaven. Then came seven generations of gods, the last consisting of the goddess Izanami and the god Izanagi. These two descended from heaven to an island of their own making. On this island they married, and eventually Izanami gave birth to the islands of Japan and all the mountains, trees, brooks, and fields found there. Not content with this miraculous birth, they produced the lovely shining goddess Amaterasu, who gave forth so much light that she was placed in heaven as the sun along with another child, her brother the moon-god.

All this was very well, but the next offspring of Izanami and Izanagi was Susa-no-wo, a stormy, cruel god who caused trouble wherever he went, so he was sent to rule the world of darkness. The next child was the fire-god, whose fiery birth caused the death of Izanami. Even in death these miraculous gods bore offspring, for out of the tears of the grief-stricken Izanagi were created other gods of nature.

Izanagi went into the underworld in search of Izanami, but after numerous terrible experiences he returned hopelessly to the heavens, never to return to earth again.

Susa-no-wo, turbulent and mischievous, jealous of his sister Amaterasu and of the gods in general, insulted everyone he could; he even ruined her rice fields and insulted her by throwing the carcass of a skinned horse through a hole in the roof of her palace. This so enraged the sun-goddess that she renounced the world and hid in a cave. The whole world was thus plunged into darkness.

The gods assembled outside the cave to try to persuade her to come out, but she would not. Finally a fat, jolly goddess danced such a comic dance before the cave that all the gods shook with laughter. This was too much for Amaterasu. Curiosity got the better of her and she peeped out. One of the gods grasped her hand firmly and drew her out the rest of the way, and light returned to the world.

The gods decided to punish Susa-no-wo by banishing him to the underworld. Susa-no-wo descended to Japan and stayed there a while; during this time he bred many gods and goddesses—spirits of rocks, earth, water, and so forth. Then he went once and for all to his exile.

Japan, however, was ruled by Susa-no-wo's sons. In order to remedy that situation, Amaterasu decided to send her grandson, Ninigi-no-mikoto, to earth. He came to earth bearing with him the divine symbols of his authority: the jewel, the sword, and the mirror. With him came a large court of craftsmen, priests, and others, who formed the ancestors for various occupations in Japan.

*Haniwa terracotta figures,
ca. 400 A.D.,
representing people and
animals of late prehistoric
Japan (Yamato)*

Ninigi-no-mikoto was supposed to have landed from heaven in Kyushu, the southernmost of the Japanese islands. By treaty with one of Susa-no-wo's sons, he received the rulership of Idzumo, a province located in the westernmost part of the Japanese main island of Honshu. This may have been the place where the Yayoi agriculturists established their biggest settlements.

Later, Jimmu, a son of Ninigi-no-mikoto, conquered much of Central Japan, particularly that region where the old cities of Nara and Kyoto are located today. According to the chronicles written down some hundreds of years later, Jimmu, thankful for the success of his conquests, honored the sun-goddess by elaborate ceremonies. This was supposed to have taken place on February 11, 660 B.C., the date accepted by the Japanese for the founding of the empire of Japan. Jimmu was therefore the first emperor, and according to tradition his descendants have ruled Japan to this day.

Archaeology and history do not think Jimmu's reign was as early as tradition makes it; nevertheless, there is no question that the emperor of Japan can trace his lineage back to an earlier period than any other presently ruling house among the kingdoms of the earth. The early traditions were written down during the ninth century in two works; the Nihongi and the Kojiki.

19

YAMATO

Shortly after the time of Christ the turbulent nomadic peoples of the eastern part of Central Asia had grown
so in population and ambition that they came into continual
conflict. The more powerful tribes attacked the weaker and
pushed them away from the best grazing lands. The defeated
tribes in turn moved in upon other tribes and seized their
lands. Everyone pushed and shoved so that the whole region
was alive with moving people: horsemen in slat armor bearing compound bows; boys driving flocks of sheep and goats;
woman at the reins of strings of oxen or horses that hauled
wagons topped with tent homes. Everyone sought freedom
from the danger of immediate invasion and good pasturage
for their flocks and herds.

These tribal movements affected many areas of Asia.
Even the Roman Empire was to feel the impact of the nomadic invaders, and the Han Empire was in continual war
with them. Japan too was invaded by men from Central
Asia.

Haniwa warrior, ca. 400 A.D.

The people of the Yayoi culture had been in contact with Korea and from that neighbor had received such things as Chinese bronze objects and probably sericulture (silk-growing). But it also appears that out of Korea came barbarian warriors who had fled from Central Asia. These warriors crossed the straits and began the conquest of Japan. Some authorities consider this invasion the basis for the legend of Ninigi-no-mikoto's coming to Japan.

The new invaders speedily moved from Kyushu to Central Honshu. They seem to have concentrated finally in a kind of peninsula at the eastern end of the inland sea. This place was called Yamato, and therefore the period in which these people lived is often called "Yamato."

The Yamato people were warlike, but they were not primitive in their culture. They seem to have been more advanced than the Yayoi people in almost every aspect of material resources. They had iron, and though they probably spent too much time making helmets and swords, they also made good farming tools. One of their favorite amulets or ornaments was the *magatama*, or tiger's claw. This was carved from a variety of hard stones and was meant to be worn on a cord around the neck. These "claws" were probably supposed to have magic properties. The stones from which

Stone "tiger's claw," pre-500 B.C.

Yamato tomb

the magatama were made included nephrite and jade, both of which are found in Central Asia but not in Japan. So they apparently still kept contact with their old homeland.

The Yamato people buried their emperors in stone chambers over which they piled great mounds of earth—just as the Scythians and other Central Asians did. Some mounds were surrounded by moats as protection from invaders. The tomb with its surrounding moats and gates covered many acres and ranks in size with some of the great monuments of antiquity.

Set in rows on the slopes and the ground around the mound tombs were *haniwa*—small terracotta statues of men, women, and animals, usually cylindrical in form. These statues have given us a clear view of part of the past: horses saddled and waiting for their riders; warriors in full armor; ladies with sleeved robes and dangling earrings; musicians strumming the samisen, a three-stringed instrument somewhat like a banjo. Some of the faces had lines of red paint as if to represent tattooing or face-painting. Together, the haniwa represented a complete court ready to serve the dead in another world. They were probably substitutes for human sacrifice.

20

JAPANESE WRITING
AND SPEECH

The Japanese language, in contrast to the Chinese, is very rich in sound. It is a melodious language so expressive that it has made Japanese poetry and drama world famous. There are Japanese words which are not intended to be translated but are used only for their sound, such as:

gusugusu—the sound of going around and around
gasagasa—the sound of rustling
barabara—falling rain

Shortly before Buddhism was introduced into Japan around A.D. 400, the Japanese did not have writing, so, as contacts with China grew, they learned Chinese writing or Kanji. However, for many reasons Chinese writing alone was not satisfactory. Chinese writing could not express the sounds of Japanese efficiently. For one thing, Japanese grammar is much more complicated than Chinese. Therefore an alphabet was devised to go with Chinese characters. This alphabet has seventy-five letters and is called *hiragana* or "running hand." Later another alphabet, *katakana* or "stiff hand," was created. This is similar to *hiragana* and is used for foreign words or official letters. In the nineteenth century when there was contact with the West and Japan became modernized, the Japanese used English or Roman letters for their language— this is called *Romaji*. Thus the Japanese have the wonderful Chinese writing to write meaning and other alphabets for sounds and other meanings. This combination of writing form and rich oral language has given the Japanese one of the most expressive means of communication in the world.

21

THE COMING
OF THE BUDDHA

Japan is a lovely country. It is, in fact, one of the loveliest countries in the world. Surrounded by the sea, covered with forested mountains, with valleys and plains of rich soil, and generally blessed with a benign climate, Japan is a good land in which to live. It is no wonder that the wanderers of Asia were thankful that they found their way there. It is this thankfulness that one feels expressed in the ancient Japanese religion called "Shinto."

As already mentioned, the Japanese legends tell of the founding of all things by the gods. Just as did the ancient Chinese, the Japanese believed that there were spirits in all aspects of nature: the rocks, trees, wind, flowers, and water. Even buildings were thought to absorb the spirit of the materials from which they were built. To this day, traditional buildings are built with this in mind. It would not do to drive a metal nail into a wooden post, for the spirit (or *Kami*) of the nail would injure the spirit of the wood. That is why wooden pegs are often used to hold a building together. Wood on wood is the rule.

The Japanese go even further in their awareness of the spirit world. In laying out a garden or choosing the site of a country house, or even in the selection of a path for a walk, the Japanese are careful to involve the world of nature. As one walks through a garden one is constantly led to quiet views of small lovely things: a gnarled tree standing by a smooth rock, a tiny waterfall falling into a small green pool, a single white flower growing before a dark green bush. In the midst of these natural things the Japanese place man-made structures meant to blend with their setting: a curving bridge causing a reflection of a perfect circle in a pool, a moss-covered stone lantern by the walk, a wooden pavilion on a point of land that seems to float on water. All these things are planned to bring harmony and permit the visitor to meditate upon the beauties of life—as if all the spirits of nature were evoked for peace. This kind of thought is very old in Japan, and it is basic to an understanding of Japanese art and character.

Buddhism, which reached Japan via China, was close to Japanese ideas developed centuries before. With its emphasis on meditation and harmony, it was readily accepted. Around A.D. 600, Crown Prince Shotoku encouraged the teaching of Buddhism so much that there were almost fifty temples in Japan, and hundreds of people were converted to the faith.

A hundred or so years later the capital of Japan was Nara, a city of Buddhist temples and monasteries. These temples still stand today. They are made of wood incredibly aged. Deep in their recesses wonderful figures of wood rest on lotus pedestals. These figures represent the beginnings of the schools of art for which Japan was to become famous and which mark the true beginnings of civilization in Japan.

PART FOUR

CENTRAL ASIA

As has been described before, China, Korea, and Japan owed much to Central Asia. It was across Central Asia that new ideas and new inventions came. Indeed, the Chinese, Koreans, and Japanese themselves have Central Asian roots. Most dramatic has been the constant movement of Central Asians over the grasslands and deserts, back and forth like the tides of the sea. Sometimes those tides broke over the Great Wall of China to fall on the settled lands beyond. Sometimes they simply moved westward out into the far regions of Turkestan and the Ukraine. But always there has been movement of men and their animals. This movement has often changed the course of history and profoundly affected the destinies of Far Eastern nations.

22

THE NOMADS

Across the middle of Asia, from central Europe almost to the shores of the China Sea, there is a wide belt of windy grassland, broken occasionally by mountains, deserts, and rivers. In ancient times these plains teemed with game: bears, boar, wolves, rabbit, birds, bison, and, most important, wild horses. In rivers like the Volga and the Oxus fish abounded, and everywhere the rich grass provided nourishment for bird and beast.

From earliest times men have hunted in these grasslands, and today archaeologists often come across the campsites of primitive hunters. But it was not until about 2500 B.C. that man began to take full advantage of the steppes, as the vast grassy plains are called.

Probably herders driving flocks of sheep and goats or herds of cattle first discovered the advantages of the grasslands. They were doubtless farmers who had found fertile soil in the river valleys and kept flocks to supplement their crops. Perhaps as they roved farther and farther from their

97

Ram's head, wooden decoration for a bridle

farms in the search for new pastures they found that they did not need to depend on grain and vegetables for food. They became nomads, whose home was wherever they found themselves. Their herds provided almost everything they required: meat, milk, and cheese for food; wool, hair, and skin for clothes and houses; bone, teeth, and horn for the manufacture of tools and ornaments; and sinew and leather for a variety of purposes. The fruits, herbs, and edible plants of the steppe provided other food and materials. When still other goods were needed they could be secured in trade at the villages or, if need be, stolen.

The small groups of herders roaming over the grasslands converted others whom they met to their way of life. They moved with the seasons according to where the grass grew. Around 2500 B.C. they began to tame the wild horses of the grasslands. By 2000 B.C. they were using heavy two-wheeled carts drawn by horses. Men began to watch over their herds from horseback.

The horse gave the people of the grasslands much more mobility than they had ever had. They could move rapidly, at will, across great distances. This boded ill for the settled peoples of the ancient world, for the wealth of cities

Bronze belt decoration,
Tagar culture, ca. 400 B.C.

and towns, and the rich pastures of the farmers, attracted the nomads. The efforts of the great civilizations to keep out the horse barbarians have filled many chapters in the story of the ancient world.

A large number of peoples of antiquity originated in the grasslands. The Aryans of India came from there, as did their relatives, the Greeks and the Persians. Many peoples of Europe, such as the Celts and the Belgians, the Hungarians and the Slavs, moved as nomadic tribes over the steppes before they finally reached the places in which they settled.

The Japanese and Korean people also have origins in Central Asia, according both to legends and to some archaeological evidence. The Chinese too owe at least their racial characteristics to ancient Central and North Asian races. But as early as the time of Confucius the Chinese tried to deny the idea that they had not always lived in China proper. Confucius himself emphasized that the roots of the Chinese were deep in the land of their ancestors and all ancient ideas as to wandering should be forgotten. Indeed, almost to this day many Chinese have abhorred such products of the herdsman as wool and milk.

With horses even the barren Gobi Desert could be used by the nomads, for whenever there was even a little rain grass would spring up and the nomads' herds could be brought there to eat and to multiply. People like the Mongols learned to time their visits to the desert to take advantage of the seasons when the grass grew. In other seasons they would migrate to the mountain slopes and grassy hills to the north and east of the Gobi, which today are the borderlands of Outer Mongolia and the Soviet Union. Indeed, along the course of the Great Wall, between it and the Gobi, are broad reaches of grassland excellent for nomadic herds.

In prosperous years, when there was much grass and the herds grew in number, the nomadic herdsmen were often quite peaceable, contenting themselves with raids upon one another or the Chinese for sport, proof of manhood, or loot. But in poor years, when the grasslands were almost desert and the herds began to die, whole tribes moved from home territories, seeking sustenance elsewhere. This brought them into conflict with other tribes, and wholesale slaughter of the defeated was not uncommon.

23

THE BARBARIANS
AND CHINA

The emphasis the Chinese placed on settled life as the best possible of all ways of life, and on the settled life of China as a high mark of civilization, made them think of their neighbors as "barbarians." There was good reason for this in the case of the Central Asians. The rich lands of China drew the Central Asian tribes in their often desperate search for sustenance as a magnet draws a nail. Their superb horsemanship and their mobility kept the border in constant turmoil, and very often terrible battles had to be fought in an attempt to make the border safe. Even the Great Wall could not keep them out. Success or failure in barbarian affairs was the measure of strength of a ruling dynasty, and Chinese history is full of accounts of the troubles each ruler had along China's Central Asian border.

Sometimes the Chinese could hold the barbarians off by giving shelter to the most powerful among them or by sending foodstuffs and providing pasturage in selected areas.

Central Asian mounted archer and horseman, from a tomb tile,
Han Dynasty

This meant treaties where an imperial princess was given in marriage to a barbarian chief or hostages were exchanged. Many were the stories told of the fate of the people who had to play such roles in ancient times.

One of the earliest peoples to invade China were the Ch'in, who brought about the downfall of the Chou Dynasty, as has been mentioned. When the Ch'in ruled China they became as Chinese as the people of Confucius' old state of Lu. Among the invading barbarians were several groups of non-Mongoloid racial stock, for there are reports of blond, blue-eyed, or red-bearded people. Some groups were more like the Turks of Central Asia today and were probably ancestral to them.

The most famous of the ancient Central Asia tribes were those people called by the Chinese "Hsiung-Nu." They probably spoke some form of the old Turkish language. One has to keep in mind the fact that Central Asian pastoral nomad tribes never numbered more than a few thousand people. Each tribe has its own traditions based on the idea that everyone in the tribe had a common ancestry in some divine or illustrious person or persons—or even an animal. Indeed, within the tribe there were subdivisions called "clans," whose members regarded themselves as brothers and acted that way even though they had no real blood connection. They would even refuse to marry a clan brother's sister since that would be like marrying one's own blood. Instead they would obtain a wife from another clan within and sometimes outside the tribe. Woman stealing was sometimes regarded as the best way to get a wife among some groups.

Among the tribes there would often appear a leader

Bronze horse, harness decoration, ca. 300 B.C.

who was able not only to obtain the complete loyalty of his own tribe, but by war or marriage to gain the leadership of other tribes. Then all these tribes together, even though some might speak a different language or have different customs, would be called by the name of the dominant tribe. Words like "Mongol" and "Hun" historically apply to such tribal confederations, and this is certainly true for the Hsiung-Nu. Such confederations lasted as long as the leader was powerful and successful in winning battles and obtaining riches. When a leader was killed or died, his son tried to succeed him in all his power, but it was rare that a son could do this. Usually the confederations broke up as contenders vied for power. Naturally the Chinese encouraged dissension among the barbarians.

The Hsiung-Nu were most powerful at the time of the Han Dynasty and fought savagely against the Han rulers

Sino-Siberian bronze deer, Ordos Desert, ca. 300 B.C.

for almost two centuries. In the end the Han were victorious, and the Hsiung-Nu, divided and defeated, faded from history only to be replaced by new barbarian forces.

Several times in Chinese history barbarian tribes completely conquered China and ruled for long periods of time. In the twelfth century it was the Mongols under Genghis Khan. When Marco Polo visited China early in the thirteenth century the emperor was Kublai Khan, grandson of Genghis Khan. The rule of the Mongols lasted until the middle of the fourteenth century.

Little is known about the Central Asian "barbarians" of the time of ancient China, but there are both ancient records and archaeological finds that tell about the Scyths who lived in western Central Asia and fought the Greeks and Persians. Their way of life was similar in many ways to what is known of the barbarians beyond the Great Wall in ancient times.

24

AT HOME IN SCYTHIA

Across the wide plain of waving grass there is a grove of trees. Smoke rising above the grove marks the presence of a settlement. As one rides nearer, the bellowing of cattle and the baaing of sheep draw attention to great herds and flocks on every side. Here and there riders busily round up strays or urge the herds toward stockades for the night.

One of the men catches sight of the traveler and races over the steppe to greet him. To the traveler from the Near East, who is used to wrap-around garments, the Scythian seems oddly dressed. On his head is a peaked hood with waving strings tied under his chin. Long, dark hair cascades from under the hood and down to his shoulders. A woolen tunic with sleeves reaches to just above the knees, and around the chest is a belt to keep the tunic closed. Tight-fitting pants are tucked into high leather boots. Evidently both tunic and pants have been made to fit the individual. Tailor-made garments of this kind would not hamper someone who spent most of his life on horseback.

As the Scythian hospitably leads the visitor toward the camp, the latter notes the peculiar bow he carries. It is made of wood backed with sinew and leather, and it is short, thick, and bent inward at the middle like a vertical yoke. The Scythian handles this bow very skillfully; its shortness and its shape permit him to launch an arrow with great force even while riding at full speed.

The camp is a strange place. Huge wagons are drawn up here and there between large tents made of felt. The wagon wheels are solid disks of wood spiked with iron, and the huge superstructure is made of felt and wood. The busy way in which people move in and out of these wagons indicates that they are used as homes just as much as are the tents.

A guide leads the visitor into one of these wagon houses. A rug flap serves as a doorway. Inside, the bright light from the firepot in the center and from the smokehole above reveals an array of rugs, carpets, and hanging tapestries richly decorated with colorful and swirling designs of horses, stags, rams, birds, and fantastic creatures. On the walls are trophies of war and the chase. A round leather shield hangs next to a silver knife embossed with exotic animal designs, and these, together with a profusion of axes, adzes, picks, swords, bridles, and vessels in bronze, iron, and even gold, indicate the wealth of the family.

The ladies of the house—a Scythian usually has more than one wife—come in from another room and make the guest comfortable. They wear wrap-around cloaks of felt with a touch of fur. As they begin to prepare the meal they remove their cloaks, revealing tailored robes reaching al-

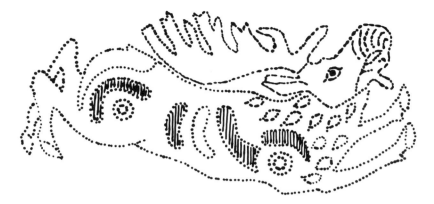

Stag, from felt saddle-cover decoration, ca. 400 B.C.

most to the floor. The sleeves are beautifully decorated with brightly colored threads, and curving designs over the bodice emphasize the lines of the figure. Their soft slippers are made of felt and fur—some of ermine. An abundance of bracelets, rings, and necklaces made of bronze, silver, and gold, complete their costumes. Perhaps these have been put on to greet the guest.

While the women prepare the meat and vegetables in a caldron the guest and his host recline on rug-covered benches. Before them are placed drinking horns filled with wine or jugs of kumiss—fermented mares' milk, a drink that produces quite an effect upon the uninitiated!

Leaning back against a cushion stuffed with deer hair, host and guest enjoy the luxury of a hot meal. Then, as the cold Asian winds sweep up in the night, sleep is sound, with a thick rug underneath and a warm felt robe as a blanket.

25

LIFE ON THE STEPPE

The Scythians were famous for their love of hunting. A story is told that once, when a Persian army under King Darius was about to attack a Scythian army, a rabbit sprang up between them and raced away. To the amazement of the Persians, the Scyths forgot all about the war and tore off after the creature. Darius could not help remarking, "Indeed, those men completely despise us."

Their pursuit of the swift animals of the steppe, using lasso as well as bow and arrow, took up many days of the year, and anyone who excelled in the chase won much prestige. Their ability to use weapons accurately while riding rapidly made them dangerous enemies.

The Scythians drew the Persians farther and farther out onto the steppes, continuing to avoid battles but harrying them on every side. Although Darius tried again and again to get them to fight a really decisive battle, they always kept just out of reach. Finally, in disgust, and perhaps some appre-

Tiger and goat, from felt saddle-cover decoration, ca. 400 B.C.

hension, the Persians retreated to the sea and from then on left Scythia alone.

Naturally the Scythians paid much attention to their horses. Boys were born to the saddle, and the need to take care of the horse was instilled in them early in life. The horses seem to have been principally small and shaggy, like most Central Asian breeds, but the taller, heavier horses of the south were bred into the line.

Most Scythians probably had two homes—winter quarters in some sheltered river valley where perhaps they built wooden shelters, and a summer encampment far out on the steppe or on the slopes of one of the high Asian mountain ranges. Because the herds needed water, drought conditions would often force the tribes to move far beyond their normal ranges. But usually there was an unwritten recognition of both tribal and familial pasturage rights which kept order among them. The Scythian laws were simple, dealing justice swiftly and efficiently.

The Scythian boy lived a hardy life in the open. Almost as soon as he could ride he was given responsibilities in the care of the herd. He had to grow in knowledge as well as in strength, learn to use a bow, brew kumiss, tan leather, make a tent, place a saddle, twirl a lasso, sense a storm, build a fire, fix a wheel, signal from afar, and a host of similar things.

A girl learned to cook, sew, weave, prepare game, milk goats, set up a home, and in general care for the camp. Since Scythian men were allowed to marry more than one wife, there were usually several female relatives from whom she could learn.

Bronze birds' heads, harness decoration, ca. 400 B.C.

The Scyths carried with them various means of entertainment, including dolls, model wagons, drums, children's weapons and tools, and probably a variety of pets. For adults there were gambling games such as dice, instruments such as drums, horns, strings, and pipes, and above all the pleasures of storytelling. Many a night, stories of the chase, of wars, and romantic love were recounted with dramatic gesture and eloquent tongue. Folk heroes and epic warriors vied with the gods in their accomplishments and pricked the imagination of this warrior people.

Most of these stories have been lost to us, but they were undeniably like those of Beowulf, Harold the Fair-haired, King Arthur, and many others of western Europe.

26

SORCERY AND RELIGION

The Scythians believed in sorcery just as did the
Koreans. Certain men among them—probably those whose
behavior made them seem "possessed"—were especially
designated to communicate with the world of spirits, which
the Scythians thought was everywhere about them and affected everyone's life. The sorcerers painted their faces and
hung odd objects like human bones and animal claws around
their necks. They carried drums, which during the rituals
they beat as an accompaniment to their chants. Sometimes
they went into frenzied fits or lay in trancelike immobility
for hours. They were highly regarded, for their duties included predicting the future and offsetting evil fortune.

Most Scythians carried amulets of some kind as a
protection against evil. These were usually acquired from a
sorcerer or a priest, who vouched for their efficacy provided
the wearer was worthy of being protected.

The future was foretold in several ways, the two most
popular being the splitting of bast fibers and the observation

Bronze stag, pole-top decoration, ca. 450 B.C.

of bundles of twigs. In the latter the twigs were probably tossed into the air and the pattern they formed when they fell was believed to indicate what the future held in store— good or bad.

Basically, Scythian religion, like most Central Asian religion, was a worship of the forces of nature. The sun, moon, stars, sky, wind, water, and earth were the principal deities. There were no temples since the people were nomadic and rarely stayed in one place for long. Instead, on religious occasions they would gather in an open place or amid a grove of trees and carry out their rituals of sacrifice, prayer, dancing, and chanting under the direction of men made priests for the ritual. Having done this, they would move on without looking back. Certain mountains or groves did have sacred meaning, however, and annually they tried to return to them to carry out certain ceremonies.

Central Asian religious feeling was revealed most awesomely in their treatment of the dead.

27

THE GREAT CHIEF
IN LIFE AND DEATH

The tribes were ruled by chiefs who were responsible for protecting the people, finding good pasturage, and in general seeing to the well being of the whole group. The chiefs gained power and prestige through physical prowess, especially in war and in the chase, and constantly sought opportunities to prove themselves.

Since so much of the success and prestige of each family and tribe depended on its men, the death of a chief or even of a father was a matter of great moment—a time for sorrow and for paying homage to the deceased.

The Central Asians believed in an afterlife where the dead would awaken and carry on their lives just as they had in this world. They felt, therefore, that it would not do for a great chief to wake from the dead and find himself without his favorite horses, attendants, weapons, and ornaments.

The Scythians constructed elaborate tombs in which all these things could be gathered together around the body of the dead chief. Usually the tomb chamber was dug into the ground, and its walls and roof were constructed of wood. The tomb itself was divided into rooms, and in the principal room the chief lay in a coffin surrounded by his weapons: shield, sword, lasso, bow and arrows, and armor. Vessels of bronze, gold, or silver, as well as bracelets, necklaces, and other ornaments were also ranged around him.

What kind of heaven would it be for a man without a wife? Sometimes a favorite wife was strangled and buried in the same coffin with her husband. More often she was laid in an adjoining room. The bodies of attendants, grooms, cooks, kinsmen, and others were placed in the other rooms—all ready to rise with their dead master and serve him as before. The bodies of horses, many of them fine steeds obviously sacrificed in their prime, have also been found.

Over these tomb chambers were raised enormous earthen mounds, called barrows, which served both as monuments and markers. Unfortunately the wealth contained in these barrows was a great temptation. Tomb robbers often broke into them and stole everything they could lay their hands on. Archaeologists have only found a few tombs left intact.

In southern Siberia, high up on the grassy slopes of the Altai Mountains, Russian archaeologists not only have found the tombs of chiefs, possibly of the Hsiung-Nu, but have found them intact. Even more remarkable is the excellent state of preservation of the remains. The ground in which these tombs were dug is frozen practically the year round. In fact, a layer of ice is frequently found between the tomb and the surface of the ground. The tomb contents are therefore set in a kind of natural deep-freeze. Some of the

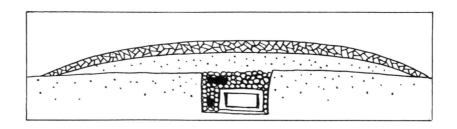

Chieftain's burial, ca. 450 B.C.

bodies are so well preserved that the tattooing with which the Hsiung-Nu, Scythians, and others loved to decorate themselves can be clearly seen. Many of the tombs date from about 500 B.C., which means that they are about 2500 years old.

Although these Central Asians lived a strenuous life they loved art and the beautiful things that could be made of rich cloth and of gold, silver, and bronze. Each of these tombs is a treasure trove of the Central Asian world. They demonstrate not only the skill of the craftsmen, but also the influences of the Chinese and Persians with whom they traded.

The contents of the tombs give us an idea of what a chief's funeral was probably like. Because people like the Scythians were able to bury their dead only twice a year—in the spring and in the fall—they used embalming. It was a crude process of opening the body, cleaning it out, stuffing it with fragrant roots and herbs, and then sewing it up again.

For forty days before the burial the deceased was carried about the land where he had once ruled. The cart bearing the body on its bier was followed by mourners shrieking their lamentations. Horsemen probably dashed about dramatizing the former prowess of the dead. His family and servants, all richly dressed, accompanied the procession, and fine horses in trappings of gold-ornamented leather and fine embroidered blankets pulled the carts that bore the belongings of the chief. Some of the horses wore masks of white felt inlaid with gold and topped with leather stag horns like plumes.

At the tomb the dead man was lowered into the main chamber and his belongings placed around him. Tapestries were hung along the walls and his clothes draped from hooks.

The body might be enclosed in a coffin made out of a hollowed tree trunk. Next the favorite wife, groom, cook, other servants and bodyguards were strangled or poisoned and placed in their coffins on the floor of surrounding rooms along with their belongings and professional instruments. Last the horses were led to points just outside the wooden tomb walls but well within calling distance of their master. There they were killed with a blow on the head. Perhaps there was a last ritual of burning incense to heaven, and then the tomb was covered over.

The new chief, having fulfilled his obligations to his predecessor, went about his duties: pastures to be found, quarrels to be settled, an enemy raid to be punished, a treaty with a neighbor to be arranged, a ritual to be carried out, a race to be run. These would fill his life until the time came when war, accident, or disease sent him to the sacred burial ground, which was the only settled place in the nomadic world of Central Asia.

CONCLUSION

China, Japan, Korea, and Central Asia are not all of the Far East. If one were to include all those lands that were directly influenced by the cultures of China alone, one would have to include the far-flung islands of Indonesia, mainland Southeast Asia, and the remote reaches of Siberia. The little described on the previous pages does small justice to the teeming world that flourished around the shores of the China Sea and the Sea of Japan before Buddhism came. Yet even an encyclopedia filled with facts would still be far short of describing just what was that ancient world. Therein is the true wonder of the Far East: as much as men learn of its accomplishments there is still more, much more, to learn!

CHRONOLOGY
BIBLIOGRAPHY
ACKNOWLEDGMENTS
INDEX

CHRONOLOGY

DATES	CHINA	KOREA
2000 B.C.	Hsia Dynasty (?)	
1700 B.C.	Shang Dynasty (ca. 1776–1122 B.C.)	
1000 B.C.	Chou Dynasty (ca. 1122–249 B.C.)	Kija Dynasty (1122–193 B.C.)
500 B.C.	Confucius (ca. 550–479) Lao-Tze (?)	
200 B.C.	Ch'in Dynasty (227–207 B.C.)	
	Han Dynasty (202 B.C.–220 A.D.)	Kingdom of Silla (57 B.C.–935 A.D.)
200 A.D.		
	Buddhism comes	Kingdom of Keguryo (55–668 A.D.) Kingdom of Paekcke (4–713 A.D.)
600 A.D.		
800 A.D.		

JAPAN	CENTRAL ASIA	DATES
Jomon culture (ca. 4500–250 B.C.)		2000 B.C.
	Prehistoric cultures	1700 B.C.
		1000 B.C.
Jimmu (first emperor, 660–585 B.C.)	Scythian rule in west	
		500 B.C.
Yayoi culture (300 B.C.–300 A.D.)	Sarmatians in west Hsiung-Nu in east	200 B.C..
Yamato (250–550 A.D.)		200 A.D.
Buddhism (ca. 575 A.D.)		600 A.D.
The Kojiki and the Nihongi		800 A.D.

BIBLIOGRAPHY

Belenitsky, Aleksandr. *Central Asia* (Archaeologia Mundi). Cleveland: World Publishing Co., 1968.

Cheng Te-k'un. *Archaeology in China.* 3 vols. Toronto: University of Toronto Press, Vol. II, *Shang China,* 1960; Vol. III, *Chou China,* 1963.

Goodrich, L. C. *A Short History of the Chinese People.* New York: Harper & Bros., 1943.

Jettmar, Karl. *Art of the Steppes.* New York: Crown Publishers, 1967.

Kidder, J. Edward. *Japan Before Buddhism.* New York: F. A. Praeger, 1966.

Koang-chih Chang. *The Archaeology of Ancient China.* New Haven: Yale University Press, 1963.

Lattimore, Owen. *Inner Asian Frontiers of China.* New York: American Geographical Society, 1940.

Osgood, Cornelius. *The Koreans and Their Culture.* New York: The Ronald Press Co., 1951.

Sansom, G. B. *A Short Cultural History of Japan.* New York: Appleton-Century Co. 1943.

ACKNOWLEDGMENTS

The quotation from Lao-Tsu on page 45 is taken from William Theodore de Bary, ed., *Sources of Chinese Tradition* (New York: Columbia University Press, 1960), p. 63.

Grateful acknowledgment is made to the following for permission to use illustrations:

PAGES 17, 35, 37, 43, 52, 67, 83, 86, 87: American Museum of Natural History, New York, N.Y.

PAGE 22: The Art Institute of Chicago

PAGES 27, 31, 41, 46: The Metropolitan Museum of Art, New York, N.Y.

PAGE 32: The William Rockhill Nelson Gallery of Art, Kansas City, Mo.

PAGE 79: M. Taeda

PAGES 69, 73: U.S. Army Signal Corps

PAGES 19, 53, 56, 58, 102: University of Toronto Press (illustrations redrawn from *Tomb Tile Pictures of Ancient China* by William Charles White)

INDEX

agriculture, 8, 10-11; Chinese, 14-17, 18; cultivation of wild plants, 8, 10; domestic animals, 17; Han Dynasty, 57; Korean, 66; plain of dust, 11
Ainu, 78, 80
alphabets, Japanese, 90-91
Altai Mountains, 117
Analects, 40
ancestor worship, 2, 21-24; Korean, 68, 69
animistic religion, 68
archaeological sites: Central Asia, 97; Lolang, 70; Scythian tombs, 117-119; Shang tomb, 33
archery, 34-35
architecture: Japanese, 2, 92; Shang, 28
art: Chinese, 8; Japanese, 93; Taoist, 44
Aryans, 99
astronomy, Han Dynasty, 58

barbarians: invasion of China, 54, 100-103, 104-105; racial origins, 103. *See also* Central Asian tribes; nomadic tribes

bear cult, 78
Belgins, 99
Beowulf, 112
Buddhism, 3, 60, 69, 72, 90, 93, 121; in Japan, 93
burials: embalming, 119; Scythian, 116-117, 119-120; Shang king, 30-33; Yamato, 88-89

calendar, Korean, 66
calligraphy, 44, 47-50
Celts, 99
Central Asia, 96-120, 121
Central Asian tribes: culture, 103-104; invasion of Japan, 85. *See also* barbarians; nomadic tribes; Scyths
Charlemagne, 3
Ch'in Dynasty, 51, 53, 103
Ch'in, state of, 51
China, 1, 6-60, 64, 93, 96, 121; geography, 7; prehistoric culture, 7-9; racial origins, 99-100; warfare with barbarians, 100-103, 104-105
China Sea, 12, 97, 121
Chinese civilization, 6, 10; and the Gobi desert, 11; origins, 9, 12

Chou Dynasty, 36-38, 51, 103; collapse, 37; feudal states, 37
civil service, Han Dynasty, 58-59
Confucianism, 42, 46, 57-58, 60, 69
Confucius, 38-42, 100
creation legend, Japanese, 81-82, 84

Darius, 109-110
domesticated animals, 17, 98, 100, 110

education: Scythian, 111; Shang, 34
embalming, 119
emperor: first Chinese, 51; first Japanese, 84
emperors of China, 24

farming, *see* agriculture
feudal states, China, 37
"Fields, gardens, houses, graves," 19-20
fishermen: Chinese, 7, 12, 13; Korean, 68

Genghis Khan, 105
geography: China, 7; Japan, 92; Korea, 71
Gobi Desert, 7, 11, 100
golden age of China, 37
government: Han Dynasty, 59, 60; Taoist, 44-45
grasslands, Central Asia, 97
Great Wall of China, 52, 54, 96, 100-101, 105
Greeks, 99, 105

Han Dynasty, 53-60, 68, 70, 85, 104-105
Hangul, 68
haniwa, 88-89
"Hermit" Kingdom, 64
Hiragana, 91
historians, Chinese, 10
Hokkaido, 78

horse-drawn carts, 98
horses, 98, 100, 110
Hsia Dynasty, 25
Hsiung-Nu, 54, 103, 104-105, 117, 119
Huang Ho (Yellow River), 11, 66
Hungarians, 99
hunting: prehistoric Chinese, 7; Scythian, 109
Hwanung legend, 66

Indonesia, 121
Inner Asia, 11, 54-55
invasion of China: by barbarians, 54, 100-103, 104-105; by the Chous, 36-37
invasion of Japan, by Central Asian tribes, 85
invasion of Korea, by Japanese, 72-73

Japan, 1, 3, 13, 64, 76-93, 96, 121; civilization, 76, 78; geography, 92; racial origins, 80, 99; religion, 92-93
Jimmu, 84
"Jomon," 78, 80

Katakana, 91
Kija legend, 67-68, 70
Koguryo, kingdom of, 71-72
Kojiki, 84
Korea, 13, 64-73, 77, 96, 121; alphabet, 68; civilization, 66; climate, 65-66; geography, 68, 71; racial origins, 99
Kublai Khan, 105
Kyongju, 72

language: Chinese, 47-48; Japanese, 90-91; Korean, 68
Lao-Tzu, 42, 45
legends: creation, Japanese, 81-82, 84; Hwanung, 66; Kija, 67-68, 70; Scythian, 112

ABOUT THE AUTHOR

WALTER A. FAIRSERVIS, JR., is professor and chairman of the Department of Anthropology and Sociology at Vassar College, Poughkeepsie, New York, and acting curator of the Eurasian Anthropology Collections at the American Museum of Natural History, New York City. Dr. Fairservis has participated in numerous archaeological expeditions in the Middle East and Far East.

He is the author of a number of books, among them *India*; *Egypt, Gift of the Nile*; and *Mesopotamia, the Civilization That Rose Out of Clay* and has written many archaeological reports and contributed to scientific journals.

Born in New York City, Dr. Fairservis now lives in Sharon, Connecticut, with his wife Jan—an illustrator who supplied the drawings used in this book—and their four daughters.